Can Music Help
Special Education Students
Control Negative Behavior
in the Classroom?

Can Music Help
Special Education Students
Control Negative Behavior
in the Classroom?

Pennie Rockerfeller

To order additional copies of this book, contact:
Xlibris LLC
1-888-795-4274
www.Xlibris.com
Orders@Xlibris.com
664884

TABLE OF CONTENTS

CHAPTER 1

NATURE OF THE PROBLEM

Music is an integral part of instruction for students with special needs because it allows all children to participate in an activity at their level and provides a sense of community for even the most disabled child (Humpal & Wolf, 2003). In today's classrooms, diverse populations of students with a wide variety of needs are often grouped together. These include students with mild to severe physical, emotional, and intellectual disabilities that are now in the classroom for a small part to most of their school day. In the past special needs students were segregated and received their education entirely separate from the remainder of the school population. Music therapy is considered a related service modality in special education (IDEA, 1977). Music therapy can play an important role in special education because many students with disabilities need special instructional treatment. Parents began demanding equal opportunity for all students, which prompted the passing of Public Law 94-142, the Education for the Handicapped Act, in 1997 (IDEA, 1997). This act was passed to ensure the education for students in the "least restrictive environment" and began the movement toward mainstreaming. In mainstreaming, special needs students participated in the regular classroom for one or more parts of the day; keeping the special education classroom as their main environment until they could be moved full time into the regular classroom (Montgomery, 2001). Special Education classes are filled with students who have several problems: economic, social, emotional, and academic. Teachers assess their classes before a plan of teaching is implemented. Special education teachers are to help change the students' behavior. The teacher is to change negative behavior into positive behavior, realizing the influence of the community in which the student lives.

Can Music Help Special Education Students
Control Negative Behavior in the Classroom?

9

SUMMARY

Teachers deal with behavioral problems, which cause the educational process to become impeded in the classroom. Research has shown that the use of classroom appropriate music help to clam these students. Music allows the student to participate in class activity at their level. According to IDEA, these students must be educated in the "least restrictive environment." This act was passed to ensure the education for students who were once institutionalized. Music integrated in the classroom provides students with concrete, hands-on experiences that are essential to developing each student's ability to reason, think, solve problems, analyze, evaluate, and enhance creativity (Houchens, 1983).

STATEMENT OF THE PROBLEM

Teachers are challenged daily with special education students. These students come to class daily with different behavioral issue. Some teachers, although trained in special education, do not have the skills necessary to accommodate these students. Music may help the teachers become better prepared for these students. Can the use of music help special education students control negative behavior in the classroom?

SOCIAL IMPLICATIONS

This study suggest how the use of background classroom music would encourage positive behavior change in the cognitive, perceptual, motor, social and emotional development of disabled students. Using this research would give teachers the necessary tools needed to help produce successful special education students. They (the teachers) would be better equipped to handle the several behavioral challenges in the classroom. Suspensions would decrease, the student would learn that challenges occur in life, but the assistance of music, which calms humans, would allow the teacher and student to use music to express their feelings.

STATEMENT OF THE PURPOSE

The purpose of this study is to suggest how the use of background classroom appropriate music encourages positive behavior change in the cognitive, perceptual, motor, social and emotional development of disabled students.

RESEARCH QUESTION

Can the use of background classroom appropriate music deter students from becoming a distraction in the educational process for themselves and others?

SIGNIFICANCE OF STUDY

The significance of this study is to prove how the use of music in the inclusion class will help the student change negative behavioral to positive decreasing the occurrences of negative results. This paper is organized accordingly (1) Does Music Really Help? ; (2) Main contributions to cognitive, biopsychosocial development of children with disabilities, (3) Implications for learning, (4) Implications for using music to accommodate students with disabilities in inclusion classes.

STUDY LIMITATIONS

1. School systems implementing music in the classroom, as part of the curricular.

2. The use of school loudspeaker to pipe music into all classes.

3. Instructing teachers on new ways of teaching.

4. Developing workshops, with the school systems approval, using Music Therapy to teach self-control, instead of suspending the student.

5. Parents must be will to allow their student to participate in the study.

6. Unbiased collection of data.

7. Willing participation of administration, teachers, students, and parents.

SUMMARY

The purpose of the Special education teacher is to be change agents. They are to help the student change their negative classroom behavior to behavior that is necessary for learning. According to research music encourages positive behavior change in the cognitive, perceptual, motor, social and emotional development of disabled students. Does the use of background music deter students from becoming a distraction in the educational process for themselves and others?

CHAPTER 2

REVIEW OF RECENT LITERATURE

Recent studies on this topic have concentrated on different aspects of learning, ranging from reading comprehension to writing ability, from mathematics problem solving to on-task performance in science classrooms. Some studies have been small-scale observational studies undertaken in the natural classroom setting, while others studied children in relatively sterile laboratory conditions. Subjects have encompassed all age ranges from kindergarten to university level, and results have been just as varied.

DOES MUSIC REALLY HELP?

Music has a way of changing our energy levels and moods. Without even thinking about it we use music to create desired moods---to make us happy, to enjoy movement and dance, to energize, to bring back powerful memories, to help us relax and focus. Research continues to be conducted to provide helpful guidelines for intentional use of music, especially in the classroom. According to Chris Boyd Brewer, Music helps us learn because it will---

- Establish a positive learning state

- Create a desired atmosphere

- Build a sense of anticipation

- Energize learning activities

- Change brain wave states

- Focus concentration

- Increase attention

- Improve memory

- Facilitate a multi-sensory learning experience

- Release tension

- Enhance imagination

- Align groups

- Develop rapport

- Provide inspiration and motivation

- Add an element of fun

- Accentuate theme-oriented unites

MAIN CONTRIBUTIONS TO COGNITIVE, BIO-PSYCHOSOCIAL DEVELOPMENT OF CHILDREN WITH DISABILITIES

Students with disabilities arrive in classes from kindergarten through high school. Effective integration of music in the content area creates a learning environment

CAN MUSIC HELP SPECIAL EDUCATION STUDENTS
CONTROL NEGATIVE BEHAVIOR IN THE CLASSROOM?

17

that makes all children want to learn. Collet (1992) reported a successful music integrated curriculum, which worked well with bilingual and special education students.

Music integration provide children with concrete, hands-on experiences that are essential to developing each child's ability to reason, think, solve problems, analyze, evaluate, and enhance creativity (Houchens, 1983). Houchens, also argues that music can be used as a tool to encourage human development in cognitive learning, perceptual, motor, social and emotional development.

IMPLICATIONS FOR LEARNING

In a related study, Lamb and Gregory (1993) share evidence that listening to music can facilitate learning to read, probably by increasing children's awareness of speech sounds, which is important in learning to "sound out" words (see, e.g., *"Music and Cognitive Achievement in Children"*, MRN, Fall 1994, I (2)).

Douglas and Willatts (1994) rep01ted a study of correlations between musical abilities and reading achievement in special education children. Seventy-eight boys and girls (average age eight years) were tested on vocabulary, reading, and spelling and also on some of their musical skills. The authors found a significant correlation between rhythm performance and both reading and spelling. Because correlations alone do not show a causal relationship, they also ran a small study on the effects of a six month program of music instruction designed to develop auditory, visual and motor skills; control students received instruction designed to develop their discussion skills (e.g., descriptive, imaginative and comparative).

According to Lamb and Gregory (1993) report that listening to music can facilitate learning to read, probably by increasing children's awareness of speech sounds, which is important in learning.

Douglas and Willatts (1994) reported on correlations between musical abilities and reading achievement. Seventy-eight boys and girls (average age eight years) were tested on vocabulary, reading, and spelling and also on some of their musical skills, e.g., ability to detect slight differences among rhythms. The authors found a significant correlation between rhythm performance and both reading and spelling. Because correlations alone do not show a causal relationship, they also ran a small study on the effects of a six month program of music instruction designed to develop auditory, visual and motor skills; control students received instruction designed to develop their discussion skills.

In his dissertation, Hedden (1971) proposed five music reaction profiles or music listening styles. These five styles are: associative, cognitive, physical, involvement, and enjoyment. Hedden hypothesized that people listen to music in a combination of five styles where all styles are present are some level, but one style is predominant. How a person listens to music may affect the possible transfer of cognitive abilities to other curricular areas.

Howard Gardner (1993) in his book *Multiple intelligences*, suggests that in classrooms of the future, teachers must realize that not all people have the same interests and abilities, and not all of us learn in the same way. Lessons need to be planned in a manner that utilizes the different intelligences we possess. In order to assess what students know teachers need to become assessment specialists and to devise ways of assessment that utilize activities that are contextualized and meaningful to students.

IMPLICATIONS FOR USING MUSIC TO ACCOMMODATE STUDENTS WITH DISABILITIES IN INCLUSION CLASSES

Special education teachers have used music to alter mood and assess emotional problems. Music allows the individual to invent emotions. Music is viewed as an integral part of all children's lives. Children enjoy listening to music, singing, and humming. Music may effectively enhance the ability for children to cope with stress in the classroom. One author suggests that music should be in both music classes and education classes. She found that integrating literature with musical content helped to bring books alive and that musical classrooms encouraged children to relate and participates in the activities (Giles, Cogan, & Cox, 1991).

Rauscher (1995) recommends engaging students in music study at early ages to involve students in an activity their already love, making noise, in order to advance their other intellectual capacities.

According to study, the inclusive classroom is founded on the belief that children should begin in the regular classroom and be moved to another environment only if proper accommodations cannot be made. Music is an integral part of instruction for students with special needs because it allows all children to participate in activities at their level and provides a sense of community for even the most disabled child (Humpal & Wolf, 2003).

Two leading authors in this arena are Renate Nummeia Caine and Geoffrey Caine (1994). They have attempted to define new approaches to teaching and learning that take into account how the brain actually functions.

Recent studies on, music have concentrated on different aspects of learning, ranging from reading comprehension to writing ability, from mathematics problem solving to on task performance in science classroom (Davidson, 1986). As educators we first assess the students before a plan of teaching is created. All students do not learn on the same level or the same pace. One of the most challenging responsibilities of the teacher in the inclusion classroom is behavioral management. There are many areas of teaching where integrating music can be highly effective.

According to Brewer (1995) there is a rich repertoire of classroom techniques that can be used simply and easily by anyone.

Two methods for using music, designed to create very different but equally effective learning environments, were developed through Lozanov's (1978) method. They are called concert. Active concert activates the learning process mentally, physically and emotionally, while passive concert is geared to place the student in a relaxed alpha brain wave state and stabilize the students' mental, physical and emotional rhythms to increase information absorption (Brewer, 1995). Both teaching methods result in high memory retention. Used together the two concerts provide a powerful learning experience. From experience, most inclusion students stay better focused in class with calm music played in the background.

According to scholarly study, music activates help students mentally, physically, and emotionally and creates a learning state that enhances the understanding of learning material. In active learning experience music creates a soundtrack for a learning activity (Brewer, 1995).

Music educators have offered evidence that music develop students' potential in many areas: especially, auditory discrimination, psychomotor coordination, memory development, expressive abilities, and critical thinking (Frega, 1977).

A study conducted by Shawn E. Mueske (1994) determined the effects of background music in a classroom. His study determined the effects of background music on attitude, achievement in the class; spent on task behavior. He found that there was a real difference in the attitude and achievement among the group who received music from the one who did not.

Another study conducted by Scott Shuler (1992) on 205 students testing the effects of major and minor modes. Minor modes gave the feelings of melancholy, mournful, gloomy, depression, while major mode most often gave the feelings of happy, sprightly, cheerful, joyous, and brightness.

SUMMARY

According to recent literature review music helps students change energy levels and moods. Without thinking about it music creates a desired mood. It can make us happy, sad, excited and even brings back to our psyche, powerful memories that help us to focus and relax.

According to Chris Boyd Brewer (1995), music helps us learn because it will-

- Establish a positive learning state

- Create a desired atmosphere

- Build a sense of anticipation

- Energize learning activities

- Change brain wave states

- Improve memory

- Facilitate a multi-sensory learning experience

- Release tension

- Enhance imagination

- Align groups

- Develop rapport

- Provide inspiration and motivation

According to Chris Brewer and his studies of the effects of music in the classroom, music could help all students become successful in their academics.

Collet (1992) reported a successful music integrated curriculum, which was successful with bilingual and special education students. Music integration provides students with concrete, hands-on experience that are essential to developing each student's ability to think and reason.

In relate studies, Lamb and Gregory (1993) share evidence that listening to music can facilitate learning to read, probably by increasing children's awareness of speech sounds, which is important to sound out words.

Douglas and Willatts (1994) reported a study correlation between musical abilities and reading achievement in special education students.

Students with disabilities arrive in classes from kindergarten through high school. Effective integration of music in the content area creates a learning environment that makes all children want to learn, according to research. Houchens (1983) argues that music can be used as a tool to encourage human development in cognitive learning, perceptual, motor, social and emotional development.

Music may effectively enhance the ability for children to cope with stress in the classroom. One author suggests that music should be in both music classes and education classes. She found that integrating literature with musical content help to bring books alive and those musical classrooms encouraged children to relate and participate in activities (Giles, Cogan, & Cox, 1991).

Chapter 3

METHODOLOGY

The study will be conducted during class time in the second three-weeks of the second semester of school. Each inclusion classroom will have no more than eighteen students per class. The students in this program will receive background music for a period of nine weeks. Additionally, subjects past exposure to classical music will be measured through responses to questions. After completing the questionnaire, and permission slip then subjects will be purposefully chosen to participate in the music study.

RESEARCH DESIGN & DATA COLLECTION

As this topic develops, the prospects of performing these types of qualitative studies become more exciting. There is value of qualitative study as part of an overall study on this topic. Data will be collected by using the pre and post test included in the appendix. The use of the decrease of suspension at Oscar Smith will also be used.

PARTICIPANTS & PROCEDURE

The subjects in the study are 180 students from Oscar Smith Middle School. The students selected are all in special education inclusion classes. This studies site and sample was purposeful selected. Individuals in this sampling will be six special education inclusion classes. The site will be Oscar Smith Middle School. This school was chosen because of the high suspension rate.

DATA COLLECTION

The study will be conducted during class time in the second three-weeks of the second semester of school. Each inclusion classroom will have no more than eighteen students per class. The students in this program will receive background music for a period of nine weeks. Additionally, subjects past exposure to classical music will be measured through responses to questions. After completing the questionnaire, and permission slip then subjects will be purposefully chosen to participate in the music study.

SAMPLE

The purpose of this sample and site is to help us understand the importance of the use of music in these classes. Keeping with the standards in choosing participants and sites, this school is rich in information necessary for this study.

VARIABLES

1. School systems implementing music in the classroom, as part of the curricular.

2. The use of school loudspeaker to pipe music into all classes.

3. Instructing teachers on new ways of teaching.

4. Developing workshops, with the school systems approval, using Music Therapy to teach self-control, instead of suspending the student.

5. Parents must be will to allow their student to participate in the study.

6. Unbiased collection of data.

7. Willing participation of administration, teachers, students, and parents.

CAN MUSIC HELP SPECIAL EDUCATION STUDENTS
CONTROL NEGATIVE BEHAVIOR IN THE CLASSROOM?

31

ANALYSIS OF DATA TECHNIQUES

According to the data collected, music significantly reduces stressful behaviors in these students. Background music has proven to have a positive effect on students who are assigned to inclusion classes. Music has been used as an effective intervention for maintaining and improving active involvement, social, emotional and cognitive skills. Music therapy has had positive effects on these students who deal with psychological stressors or physiological complications. Thus, it has been researched and proven that students who receive music therapy over a long period of time have a success rate that is higher than those students who receive music therapy over a shorter period. Long-term music therapy indicates that music sessions were most effective in increasing self-control, relaxation and comfort levels inside the classroom, allowing more time for teaching.

SUMMARY

Music therapy has been researched and found to have a calming relaxing effect on students who fear large crowds, especially in classrooms. Music therapy has been proven to have a calming effect on those students who display signs of distress, or who have been diagnosed with psychological or physiological disorders. Some students show stress when taking tests. Research has proven that music significantly reduces stressful behaviors in these students. Background music has proven to have a positive effect on students who are assigned to inclusion classes. Music has been used as an effective intervention for maintaining and improving active involvement, social, emotional and cognitive skills. Music therapy has had positive effects on these students who deal with psychological stressors or physiological complications. Thus, it has been researched and proven that students who receive music therapy over a long period of time have a success rate that is higher than those students who receive music therapy over a shorter period.

Long-term music therapy indicates that music sessions were most effective in increasing self-control, relaxation and comfort levels inside the classroom, allowing more time for teaching.

BIBLIOGRAPHY

Brewer, C. (1995). Music and Learning: Seven Ways to Use music in the classroom. Tequesta, Florida: LifeSounds.

Caine, R.N., and Geoffrey, C. (1994). Making Connections. Menlo Park. Addison Wesley.

Collett, M. J. (1992). Music as the Basis for Learning. The Education Digest. May 1992: 61-4.

Davidson, C. W., & Powell, L.A. (1986). Effects of easy-listening background music on The on-task-performance of fifth-grade children. Journal of Education Research, 80(1), 29-33.

Douglas, S., & Willatts, P. (1994). The relationship between musical ability and literacy skills. Journal of Research in Reading, 17(2), 99-107.

Frega, A. L. (1997). Musica y educacion: objetivos y metodologia [Music and education: Objectives and methodologies]. Buenos Aries.

Gardner, H. (1993). *Multiple Intelligences*. New York: Basic Books.

Giles, M. M., Cogan, D., & Cox, C. (1991). A music and art program to promote emotional health in elementary schools children. Journal of Music Therapy, 2 8, 13 5-148.

Gregory, A.H., & Lamb, S.J. (1993). The relationship between music and reading in beginning readers. Journal of Educational Psychology, 13, 19-26.

Hedden, S. K. (1971). A multivariate investigation of reaction profiles on music listeners and their relationships with various autochthonous and experiential characteristics. (Doctoral Dissertation, The University of Kansas). Dissertation Abstracts International, 32.

Houchens, C.J. (1983). A personal adjustment curriculum for secondary behaviorally disordered students. Paper presented at the Minnesota Conference on Programming for the Development needs of Adolescent with Behavioral Disorders. Minneapolis, MN.

Humpal, M., & Wolf, J. (2003). *Music in the inclusive environment.* Young Children, 58, 103-107.

IDEA (1997). The Individuals with Disabilities Act Amendments of 1997. Retrieved March 9, 2008 from Web site: *http://www.ideapractices.org.*

Imig, S., & Koppelman, D. (1995). *The effects of music on children's writing content.* University of Virginia, Charlottesville, Va. (ERIC Document Reproduction Service No. (383 002).

Lozanov, G. (1978). *Suggestology and Outlines of Suggestopedy.* New York: Gordon & Breach.

Montgomery, J. (2001). Reaching special learners: From exclusion to inclusion Music Express. 1(4): 46-45.

Mueske, S. E. (1994). The Effects of Background Music in an Introductory Biology Laboratory. Mankato State University,

Rauscher, F. (1995). *Music and spatial task performance.* Nature. 365, 40-4 1.

Shuler, S. (1992). Reaching At-Risk Students Through Music Education. NAACP Bulletin. May 30-5.

Appendix A

PERMISSIONS

Dear Parents,

Our school requires parental permission for student's participation in a special project. Your son/daughter will be part of this project where background music will be played the entire class period. The purpose of this study is to show how music has a positive effect of on students' emotional, behavioral and academic progress in the class. We believe that the backgrotmd music will allow the student to become more focus. We also believe, along with hands-on activities such as reading, in-class discussion groups assist students with their different needs.

Thank you for taking the time to read and sign this permission form.

Sincerely,

_____

   Principal/Teacher

Student Name_____

_____ Yes, I give my son/daughter permission to be part of this project.

_____ No, I do not give my son/daughter permission to be part of this project.

_____

Guardian signature/date

Appendix B

PRE AND POST QUESTIONNAIRE
FOR THE TEACHER

DIRECTIONS: READ AND PUT A CHECK BESIDE THE OPTION THAT DESCRIBES YOU.

1.   Learning is truly enhanced by incorporating music.

_____ **strongly agree**

_____ **agree**

_____ **disagree**

_____ **strongly disagree**

2. There is relationship between music and memory.

_____ **strongly agree**

_____ **agree**

_____ **disagree**

_____ **strongly disagree**

3. Test scores reflect better memorization of material when a song is used as a vehicle for language learning.

_____ **strongly agree**

_____ **agree**

_____ **disagree**

_____ **strongly disagree**

4. The syntactical structure contained in the lyrics to a song is transferred to students' everyday use of the language.

_____ **strongly agree**

_____ **agree**

_____ **disagree**

_____ **strongly disagree**

5.   Music had the power to motivate students and create

a positive and relaxing environment in the classroom.

_____ **strongly agree**

_____ **agree**

_____ **disagree**

_____ **strongly disagree**

APPENDIX C

LESSON PLAN

Instructional Goals:

* Students will begin to understand how pieces of music are constructed and the different parts that make up a song

* Students will work in pairs to construct unique songs

Materials:

* Paper

* Different instruments (drum, flute, recorder, organ, maracas, etc)

Anticipatory Set:

1. The teacher will play part of a popular song to the class. After the class has listened to the song once, the teacher will play it again. This time, the class will be instructed to listen carefully to find a pattern in the music.

2. After the students describe what they think the pattern (s) may be, the teacher will give the students some definitions of what a pattern is. The teacher will also explain to the children that music actually consists of many parts, the pattern being one of the most important. Then, the teacher will play some simple patterns on different instruments. The teacher should also give volunteers the chance to try.

Activities:

1. The teacher will ask the students to pair themselves up with a partner. Then, the teacher will pass out different instruments to each pair of students.

2. Next, the students will be instructed to work together to produce a song. They will need to use the instrument to make up a pattern, and then they will need to make up words to a short song about school that will go along with the music.

3. Students should be given about a half an hour to complete this project.

4. When all the students have finished their songs, each group will come up to the front of the room to perform their song. The rest of the class will try to imitate the performing group's pattern with their own instruments.

5. If other teachers will permit, the class may take their show to other classrooms to perform.

6. If time permits, the students can brainstorm different commercials that they know that have patterns, atld they can try to play them with the instruments.

Teacher's Role:

The teacher's role in this activity is to inform the students about patterns in music. Once the teacher has helped the children to recognize the parts and patterns of music, the children should use their own creativity to produce their own songs.

Troubleshooting:

* Students may choose to use the instruments for purposes other than the assigned project. If this occurs, tell the students that they have a fun twist to their assignment- one student needs to write the words and the other needs to compose the music, but they cannot put them together until their performance.

APPENDIX D

STUDENT EVALUATION COLLECTED
FROM THE TEACHER

DIRECTIONS: READ AND PUT A CHECK BESIDE
THE OPTION THAT DESCRIBES YOUR FEELINGS.

1.   Students work well with another student.

     _____ **yes**

     _____ **no**

     _____ **do not know**

2.   They completed all assignments

_____ **yes**

_____ **no**

_____ **do not know**

3.   Students learned to use music to relax and be excited about learning.

_____ **yes**

_____ **no**

_____ **do not know**

Appendix E

PRE AND POST QUESTIONNAIRE
FOR THE STUDENTS

DIRECTIONS: READ AND PUT A CHECK BESIDE THE OPTION THAT DESCRIBES YOU.

1. Patterns work within songs to make you feel a certain way.

    _____ **strongly agree**

    _____ **agree**

    _____ **disagree**

    _____ **strongly disagree**

2.   Learning is truly enhanced by incorporating music.

_____ **strongly agree**

_____ **agree**

_____ **disagree**

_____ **strongly disagree**

3.   There is relationship between music and memory.

_____ **strongly agree**

_____ **agree**

_____ **disagree**

_____ **strongly disagree**

4.   Test scores reflect better memorization of material when a song is used as a vehicle for language learning.

_____ **strongly agree**

_____ **agree**

_____ **disagree**

_____ **strongly disagree**